This Lesson Book Belongs to:

_____

Date Started: _____

Date Finished: _____

level one

How to Use This Book

As a busy mom of 15, I'm always looking for ways to streamline my life, especially when it comes to homeschooling.

This is why I created the book you hold in your hand.

I'm also a real fan of the simple way Charlotte Mason (a Christian educator from the 19th century) approached language arts. Here it is in its essence:

Copywork

The copying of well-written prose or poetry in order to reinforce excellent spelling, grammar, and penmanship.

Narration

A "telling back" of what has been read (or read from). This is typically oral or written, but can be drawn as well.

Dictation

A measured portion (usually brief) of good literature is first studied and then dictated to the child as he writes it down.

level one
The Lesson Book

Sherry K. Hayes

One of the sweetest aspects of her ideas is that they can be applied to almost any piece of literature, which includes everything from Dr. Seuss to the McGuffey readers, to Shakespeare, to the Bible, and beyond!

This method is genius because it does away with all of those tedious reading comprehension questions and spelling lists. Even vocabulary and grammar are learned naturally if Mason's simple ideas are practiced *consistently.*

While this is truly liberating, the logistics of putting it into practice are *not*. Especially for those of us who are teaching three or more children at a time.

With this in mind, I set out to create a tool which could help moms like me.

"The Lesson Book" is not a workbook. Workbooks ask specific questions and require specific answers.

The pages I have created here are not about specifics, just about providing a framework so that you, the teacher, have less work to do.

YOU decide what needs to be copied and dictated, and your child decides what is important enough to be recorded.

Also, this recording can be done in more than one way. Besides the written word, there are plenty of spaces for drawings and doodlings (or anything else you want to add, such as a clipping of a picture or a bunch of stickers).

In this way it becomes less of a "schoolbook" and more of a memory-keeper for actual learning.

This level is for those children who are beginning to understand the basics of word composition and are sounding out simple

sentences. I love to use this one with the McGuffey's *Pictorial Eclectic Primer* and McGuffey's *First Eclectic Reader* (original version from Mott Media), but you could also use it with a simple book such as Dr. Seuss' *Hop on Pop*.

Here's how:

As you read a book and/or have the child read to you, pull out a few words for copying. You will want to write each simple chosen word carefully in the top portion of each section on the first page, leaving the bottom portion for your child to copy. (I like to use pen so that my portion doesn't get erased by accident).

To make it more fun and to aid in memory imprinting, have him draw a simple picture representing each word.

After the lesson or story is read, have your child orally tell you what it was about. Then have him draw a picture illustrating some scene, person, or important idea from the lesson.

Next, you can take a simple sentence McGuffey or Seuss wrote for the "copywork" section and write it out carefully in pen, leaving a blank line under each line you write. The child then copies it after you.

Finally, after you have gone over the sentence and explained and practiced the words included, you can dictate the sentence to the child and have him write it down as carefully as possible.

(**Note:** Be careful here. While it's a good idea to emphasize completeness and carefulness, don't allow your own need for perfection rule. Look into the heart of your little one and see the eagerness to please and make sure you praise the effort made).

You don't have to do all of this in one day. You can split the activities up over your entire week.

If you are like me, you need something visual before you can get an idea nailed in your mind. That's why we've included some actual examples (created with the McGuffey's) on the following pages.

If you would like even more explanation and ideas on true learning, make sure and visit my site, Mom Delights (momdelights.com).

I pray this small tool will bless you and your children as you enjoy your learning journey together!

Please Note: There are enough pages included here for 30 lessons. You may need more than one book to complete an entire McGuffey reader.

Example Pages:

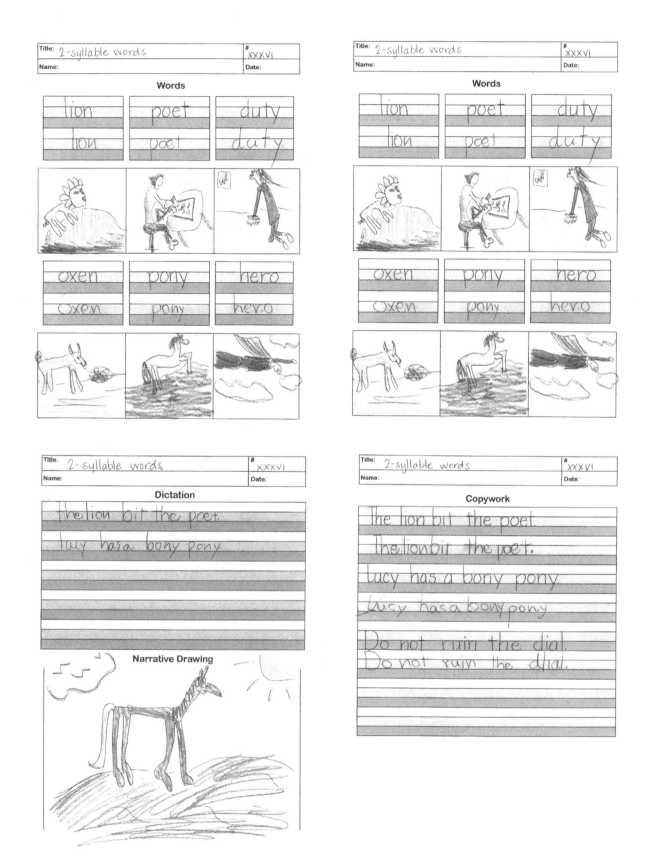

The Lessons

Title:	#
Name:	Date:

Words

Title:	#
Name:	Date:

Words

Title:	#
Name:	Date:

Copywork

Title:	#
Name:	Date:

Dictation

Narrative Drawing

Title:	#
Name:	Date:

Words

Title:	#
Name:	Date:

Words

Title:	#
Name:	Date:

Copywork

Title:	#
Name:	Date:

Dictation

Narrative Drawing

Title:	#
Name:	Date:

Words

Title:	#
Name:	Date:

Words

Title:	#
Name:	Date:

Copywork

Title:	#
Name:	Date:

Dictation

Narrative Drawing

Title:	#
Name:	Date:

Words

Title:	#
Name:	Date:

Words

Title:	#
Name:	Date:

Copywork

Title:	#
Name:	Date:

Dictation

Narrative Drawing

Title:	#
Name:	Date:

Words

Title:	#
Name:	Date:

Words

Title:	#
Name:	Date:

Copywork

Title:	#
Name:	Date:

Dictation

Narrative Drawing

Title:	#
Name:	Date:

Words

Title:	#
Name:	Date:

Words

Title:	#
Name:	Date:

Copywork

Title:	#
Name:	Date:

Dictation

Narrative Drawing

Title:	#
Name:	Date:

Words

Title:	#
Name:	Date:

Words

Title:	#
Name:	Date:

Copywork

Title:	#
Name:	Date:

Dictation

Narrative Drawing

Title:	#
Name:	Date:

Words

Title:	#
Name:	Date:

Words

Title:	#
Name:	Date:

Copywork

Title:	#
Name:	Date:

Dictation

Narrative Drawing

Title:	#
Name:	Date:

Words

Title:	#
Name:	Date:

Words

Title:	#
Name:	Date:

Copywork

Title:	#
Name:	Date:

Dictation

Narrative Drawing

Title:	#
Name:	Date:

Words

Title:	#
Name:	Date:

Words

Title:	#
Name:	Date:

Copywork

Title:	#
Name:	Date:

Dictation

Narrative Drawing

Title:	#
Name:	Date:

Words

Title:	#
Name:	Date:

Words

Title:	#
Name:	Date:

Copywork

Title:	#
Name:	Date:

Dictation

Narrative Drawing

Title:	#
Name:	Date:

Words

Title:	#
Name:	Date:

Words

Title:	#
Name:	Date:

Copywork

Title:	#
Name:	Date:

Dictation

Narrative Drawing

Title:	#
Name:	Date:

Words

Title:	#
Name:	Date:

Words

Title:	#
Name:	Date:

Copywork

Title:	#
Name:	Date:

Dictation

Narrative Drawing

Title:	#
Name:	Date:

Words

Title:	#
Name:	Date:

Words

Title:	#
Name:	Date:

Copywork

Title:	#
Name:	Date:

Dictation

Narrative Drawing

Title:	#
Name:	Date:

Words

Title:	#
Name:	Date:

Words

Title:	#
Name:	Date:

Copywork

Title:	#
Name:	Date:

Dictation

Narrative Drawing

Title:	#
Name:	Date:

Words

Title:	#
Name:	Date:

Words

Title:	#
Name:	Date:

Copywork

Title:	#
Name:	Date:

Dictation

Narrative Drawing

Title:	#
Name:	Date:

Words

Title:	#
Name:	Date:

Words

Title:	#
Name:	Date:

Copywork

Title:	#
Name:	Date:

Dictation

Narrative Drawing

Title:	#
Name:	Date:

Words

Title:	#
Name:	Date:

Words

Title:	#
Name:	Date:

Copywork

Title:	#
Name:	Date:

Dictation

Narrative Drawing

Title:	#
Name:	Date:

Words

Title:	#
Name:	Date:

Words

Title:	#
Name:	Date:

Copywork

Title:	#
Name:	Date:

Dictation

Narrative Drawing

Title:	#
Name:	Date:

Words

Title:	#
Name:	Date:

Words

Title:	#
Name:	Date:

Copywork

Title:	#
Name:	Date:

Dictation

Narrative Drawing

Title:	#
Name:	Date:

Words

Title:	#
Name:	Date:

Words

Title:	#
Name:	Date:

Copywork

Title:	#
Name:	Date:

Dictation

Narrative Drawing

Title:	#
Name:	Date:

Words

Title:	#
Name:	Date:

Words

Title:	#
Name:	Date:

Copywork

Title:	#
Name:	Date:

Dictation

Narrative Drawing

Title:	#
Name:	Date:

Words

Title:	#
Name:	Date:

Words

Title:	#
Name:	Date:

Copywork

Title:	#
Name:	Date:

Dictation

Narrative Drawing

Title:	#
Name:	Date:

Words

Title:	#
Name:	Date:

Words

Title:	#
Name:	Date:

Copywork

Title:	#
Name:	Date:

Dictation

Narrative Drawing

Title:	#
Name:	Date:

Words

Title:	#
Name:	Date:

Words

Title:	#
Name:	Date:

Copywork

Title:	#
Name:	Date:

Dictation

Narrative Drawing

Title:	#
Name:	Date:

Words

Title:	#
Name:	Date:

Words

Title:	#
Name:	Date:

Copywork

Title:	#
Name:	Date:

Dictation

Narrative Drawing

Title:	#
Name:	Date:

Words

Title:	#
Name:	Date:

Words

Title:	#
Name:	Date:

Copywork

Title:	#
Name:	Date:

Dictation

Narrative Drawing

Title:	#
Name:	Date:

Words

Title:	#
Name:	Date:

Words

Title:	#
Name:	Date:

Copywork

Title:	#
Name:	Date:

Dictation

Narrative Drawing

Title:	#
Name:	Date:

Words

Title:	#
Name:	Date:

Words

Title:	#
Name:	Date:

Copywork

Title:	#
Name:	Date:

Dictation

Narrative Drawing

Title:	#
Name:	Date:

Words

Title:	#
Name:	Date:

Words

Title:	#
Name:	Date:

Copywork

Title:	#
Name:	Date:

Dictation

Narrative Drawing

Made in United States
Troutdale, OR
02/19/2024

17812144R00073